The Next

A Book of Poetry

Caleb C-Mo Morris

THE NEXT STEP IN EVOLUTION

First edition. January 1, 2024.

ISBN: 979-8223249726

Written by Caleb C-Mo Morris.

Table of Contents

I dedicate this book to those of you who supported me with my first book. At times I lose motivation, but having genuine support has made every moment of it worth it. So thank you, I will continue to give you only the best; It's what you deserve <3

I Don't Have A Name

i don't have a name
apparently you know me
i've been called many things
my name is not one of them.
i've been asked about where i align,
in case i don't have a name,
a label will be assigned
at birth, i'm already given a number to identify
my name is not a team name,
my name is individual.
my name is not my party,
my name is not political.
my name's not my successes
my name is not my failure.
my name isn't the same,
just because we look familiar.
no, but you will call me by my name.
not the one you've given me,
but the one that i gave
Caleb C-Mo Morris

Time Heals

they say time heals,
i'm still waiting
my sorrow kills my impatience
unwanted thoughts; intrusive invasions
like rain, tears spill - the waters wading
my time is wasting
i'm still not praying
for the day i say the sorrow's fading
tomorrow's waiting with open arms
i'm learning to let go, evading harm
i may get knocked down
i'll soar, cus i'm a shooting star
if we didn't face challenges
everything else would feel hard
i'm healing; though it's hard to tell
you can't see the bruising of my mental scars
i fear that time isn't healing;
i'm simply inured to what i once couldn't stand

You're Alive, But Have You Lived?

breathing's not a choice,
you don't decide to do it
your lungs function on their own volition
so yes you're alive, but have you lived?
do you explore?
many men reflect; to deplore on their deathbed
when life's unsure, it's clear that we want to do more
are we alive or simply a corpse scraping feet along the floor?
with each step, with each breath, are we striving for more?
are we simply on autopilot with no drive
no kick in our step; no jive
"i'm surviving",
you do that every day you wake up, eat, and go to sleep
is the highlight of your life that you merely survived?
i refuse to be joy-deprived
i'm glad you survived, but that's a given
i know you're alive, but are you living?

I Don't Owe Nobody Nothing

my credit card paid off,
i have no debt that i'm dumping
there's no loan to my name
i owe nobody nothing
i pay my dues when they're true
i didn't get here on my own
i give credit when it's due
there's not a soul that is owed
i said what i meant
i have no reason to lie
the explanation was stated
i owe nobody a dime
i keep myself in good standing
its that way because of planning
i'm not in debt to you
you have no reason to demand me
you're not the lender
for i don't borrow
i refuse to be in debt
i paid in full for a better tomorrow

Step Back From Setback

you only face a setback if you step back
for moving forward opens doors worth more than yours before
"where one door closes, another opens"
not always
though a closed door isn't inherently bad.
we face a quagmire when instead of looking for open doors,
we knock on the same locked ones waiting for a different result.
the one who searches for open doors achieves more than those who
wait for a single door to open
the one with the most success turns every handle,
seeking not only every open door,
but every unlocked one.
read this again, thinking about doors as opportunities.

Look Through My Prescriptive Lens

looking through my eyes like you're looking through a camera
would probably bring discomfort for the fact i'm outta focus
i suppose having the understanding that i can't see because of light
made me pay more attention when i had the sight
you must remember i can't see forever
occasionally the contacts are returned to their case
and my glasses are set on top of something
it will probably be my second task of the day
but maybe it's for that reason i have to thank
with less vision, i focused my senses;
did more listening
its almost crazy how much you can still see with your eyes closed
you can see the dinner being cooked on the stovetop
because your nose will look for the trails until the scent stops
you can see the birds in the morning singing like they're in the shower
because taking time to listen is like another superpower
i don't necessarily meditate but sometimes i close my eyes and search
my surroundings,
listening for anything.
smelling for anything,
because when my eyes are open
my mind is scoping to see if the coast is clear
im hyperaware of the perimeter and the whole area
but as someone who is always using their senses and being aware
i often listen to things other people couldn't hear
i heard screaming the other day
and no one that's near heard some of the same
look through my lens, no it's not perfect
but you would see a lot more cus i'm observant

you would see tendencies exposing the opposite of who people pretend to be
you would see hypocrisy from those who boast cockily
you would see the self-awareness unapparent
flaws spit from the jaws of folks feeling they're above the boss
i see a lot of the bad but see as much of the good
i see the tender-hearted nature of those misunderstood
where some see thieves, i recognize someone who will eat by any means
when food is a daily quest and survival's not guaranteed
elsewhere i recognize kindness in those who purport a hard front
as if they wouldn't bend backwards any time of the month
i see the burdens, maybe pain, through the eyes of those who don't complain
with my own eyes & ears,
i watch in silence with observation
as the world around me passes by each conversation

Feeling My Feelings Fully

not for a moment will i fake what i feel;
i care to be authentic and deal with the real
if imma be mad; it's real anger
real danger; broken glass
if for only a moment i were to channel the wrath hell has
but when i'm feeling joyful with zeal
i want to jump, play, and squeal, i think;
in my curiosity lives the child i'll always be
i experience sadness too;
i made playlists for it
if we didn't have bad days
we wouldn't have good ones
so i'm grateful for it
i love as though i'll never get the chance to do it again
i curate my love like a handpicked playlist
most days are equanimous
that's where i find peace
in mind; i'm rather serious
about the balance i keep
my face speaks first
may as well feel the emotions
i grew up nonchalant
all my actions are chosen
for instance fear fails to appear in the face of danger
for the same reason i'm slow to anger
i choose which to use
as well as when and where
i couldn't make it safely if all i felt was scared
the two things that override me are disgust and surprise
shock has wide eyes staring like deer in headlights

internally mind's silent; intaking and that's all
disgust has narrow eyebrows and a scrunched-up nose

Peaceful Confidence

we all have a spirit, a soul
a heart, metaphorically
a place deep down where we exist only to ourselves
some of us... are free spirits,
who let our inner selves roam freely
some of us are confined; if not by the world...
by us.
scared to let ourselves be ourselves
some of us yearn to be free spirits;
remaining locked away in the cocoon of societal expectations
pressured by the weight of others;
whether we realize it or not, it's on us,
to decide whether we turn to diamonds or dust
many of us are able to share pieces of our soul
thanks to the security of our confidence
and the freedom of our vulnerability
confidence is the veil of invincibility withstanding the pressure that forms diamonds
arrogance is the inverse;
it begins with a confined spirit seemingly trapped in a cell
with the illusion of a diamond; merely a hollow shell
scared to share for fear of exposing internal integrity
arrogance is loud and flashy to compensate for the lack of security

Distorted Reflection

you won't see yourself when candid
all you see are distorted mirrors and cameras
you don't believe compliments
you don't know you're heaven-sent
beauty is in the eyes of the beholder
not your eyes, but mine, holding onto your beauty
perception is only your reflection of who you'd rather be

Rainy Resistance

i don't mind spending my day in the rain
unlike the previous years
no gloomy weather engenders pain
why let the rain be my tears
when i could enjoy splashing in puddles
loving, laughing, staying out of all trouble
carefree, no reactions, and forgetting the struggles we bare
being a kid again,
i lived to have fun, and walk around with no fear
finally feeling that once again in my older years

Silent Screams

we say
actions speak louder than words
yet at times
when we use neither
the silence screams

Deafening Silence

a chaotic mind
finds no peace in silence
with nothing but invasive thought
the stillness rocks the mental
like a small boat through turbulent seas

Monetary Dreams

every now and again
i'll get tight about my money
i'll remember that living the american dream is something done while asleep
that every dream i want to pursue is unattainable
unless i can find ways to make it monetary
i don't need handouts,
i'm really not here to complain
but i can't stand to live a life that don't fulfill me

Dear Future Me

dear future me,
please don't criticize me too hard
i'm trying too
i know you want the best for you
but everything i'm doing
allows for everything you want to do
i'll take care of me
i know you're doing the same now
maybe your practices are better
i'm just doing what i know how
i consider myself clairvoyant
but hindsight is much clearer
keep being a student of life
let my mistakes be your teacher
since you're applying your expectations on me
allow me to follow suit

Unapologetically Me

i live unapologetically
i wouldn't dare be sorry for being me
i'm unashamed of who i am
shame is assigned by the judgment of others

Real Ones Don't Die

they say real ones don't die
but if i go
would i feel that somebody lied
is the sentiment coming from pride
how could i possibly be any less
than every moment i was alive
they say real ones don't die
well it must be true
when you real you must be bulletproof
i got nun to lose
i got nun to prove
when i meet my dues,
i'm no less
they say real ones don't die
so i don't fear death
i don't feel stress
no use in me losing my breath
if you don't respect me alive
you not gon respect me in death
when i'm real throughout my life
then was i not real til the end?
they say real ones don't—
they don't live until the end of time
do you lose credibility when you die?
we all must go so when we do
does it matter how hard we even try
in death we all reach the same conclusion
was "real life" just a poor illusion
am i fake someday when my life slips away
or do we fall victim to delusion

there are poets we still quote
no matter how long ago the pen wrote
artists with paintings we still admire
what we appreciate won't expire
art alleviates pain and inspires
even when we move on or choose to retire
songs always outlast their singers
bees never outlast their stingers
doesn't mean we disregard their honey
just cus a doctor's gone doesn't mean his medicine can't heal
long story short;
just cus the physical body's not present
doesn't mean we're no longer real

What's In A Word?

it's just a word
or so they say
but it's far more than a word when it's used in rage
it's more than a word when you want to speak with thunder
you wouldn't say it's just a word when you sought to keep us under
asking "isn't it just a word?"
then i suppose retaliate is just a verb
let me guess, our reaction is worse
than the immediate action of words
you strung together hoping it'd hurt
"so we can't use words now?"
sometimes i laugh thinking of it as a noun
don't call me out of my name
that's a word they used to keep us down
but 400 years ago is not today
if the words slip past your lips don't stick around
you may think it's a joke, we don't think the same
i guess anything is just a word if you're reckless
if we could eliminate context completely
but there's a difference between being careless
and speaking freely
i speak my mind but i'm not senseless
and nothing's just a word but i guess
if you've never read into intention
i'll offer this as your first lesson
to ameliorate the questions
for the persistent answers you seem to have never heard
some words aren't meant to be said
then again,
its not just a word

I Am At Peace

i am at peace
in solitude
where the quiet things roam
my thoughts enact a moment of silence
alike rivers and wind flow
i have no destination
im content wherever i go
my peace can't be disrupted
i am in control
i place all the trust i owe
in mind, body, and soul

Don’t Walk In My Footsteps

don't walk in my footsteps
you don’t need to fill my shoes
i’ve uncovered most the puzzle
its on you to heed the clues
i won't make you do it
go ahead, you’re free to choose
walk alongside my steps
and when i reach the end,
walk past my footsteps,
create your own path
don’t honor me by following my footsteps
honor me by creating your own, next to mine
eventually your footsteps will be traced back to me
that’s when i’ll say;
i’m honored to have you by my side
fill your own shoes, don’t fill mine

Self-Destruction

greed led him to his own destruction
death by his own desires

Fear

sometimes it feels like it's the essence of our very being
we're scared to take a risk and chase our dreams
maybe the fear isn't eternal
what are we really afraid of?
fear itself?

a letter THat cAptures a word, a true frieNd KnowS

A friend who celebrates when you're winning and works with you when you're losing
Loving you at your best & worst. for a true friend's love is unconditional.
A fidus achates worth fighting for
Not leaving your side through turmoil but planting the bond in strong soil
Determined. not only for themselves, but for the betterment of those surrounding.
Everybody at the table eats. no one is unaccounted for unless they get up from the table and walk out the door.
Real people are hard to find, but you stand out still. the diamond in the rough, the needle in the haystack. when you're as kind as you are, inactivity is considered mean by others.

Knock The Hustle

love is wanting more for someone than they want for themselves
has my personal escape turned to my personal hell?
am i a caged bird?
my cell is workin too well
a victim of my hustle am i too locked in?

Smile

no matter what the rest of your outfit looks like,
you can always wear a smile

Little Bubble

little did he know
he was kept inside a bubble
no one had the heart to burst it
when it finally popped it was too late
he had drifted too far

Thankful

i'm thankful for the authentic who chose to be themselves,
despite the world saying they shouldn't dare
i'm thankful for the champions of peace who showed love when hate
was easier
i'm thankful for the kind-hearted who correct without being critical;
who say: "hey, there's a better way", without judgment
i'm thank for the trailblazers who made a way where there wasn't one
i'm thankful for the rays of light who let their light shine even brighter
in the darker times
i'm thankful for supporters who show up,
because being there is all the difference that's needed
your presence changes the atmosphere
i'm thankful for helpers who remind us that we aren't alone - we will
have help
i'm thankful for lifes' journeys and aligning me on the path of those
i'm thankful for,
i'm grateful for whom i've met;
and excited to meet many more!

Seasonal Depression

i've felt you creeping up on me for some time now
you're not as slick as you may hope to be
nonetheless your stealth won't matter much
if you find a way to overtake me anyways
how do i plan for something i can't see
escape what i can't hope to outrun

How It Feels To Stand Here

i stand in front of everyone
and i shake
i'm not afraid, i'm eager
i've felt this feeling before
i know it as the feeling of the starting line
ahhh, track
when i'm in my blocks
my legs shaking
ready to take me further
my arms telling me they can't wait to get out of here
but here i am,
not with eyes on the finish line
but on you, or more realistically my phone
but let's pretend we're making eye contact
we'll smile as if your eyes caught mine in passing
i can feel my body's fight or flight
but i will stand here,
i will not run
and i don't think i can take you all at once
so i'll read my poems and hope for peace

Nature:

An attestation to the greatest teacher; Mother Nature. She's incredibly consistent, you can practically count on it. Nature serves as a guide and has shown us the way of life for as long as any of us have been present. I find that if we struggle to find the answer to something we may be able to find it by observing the elements and even animals!

The Trees Are Bare

the trees are bare;
as though there were no parent prompting to grab a coat
the skies are blue;
they're fond of the sea, lost in oceans of emotion
the air is cold while the sun is out,
temperature betrays the climate;
far too cold to submit to the longing warmth
the range of goosebumps along my arms
live vicariously through the snowcaps witnessed in the distance
the morning is still,
waiting for the right time to make its move
there's a light breeze through my environment,
gently presenting a harsher condition

Snapping Twigs

the moment a twig snaps
is when its elasticity is tested
not when it's bent a little,
when it's bent a lot.
a dry twig will snap at the smallest inconvenience.
a well-watered twig, attached to a tree, is stable.
more nutrients, more flexibility.

Tipping points. 12/16/22 C-Mo! (The Writing Behind It)
i think in most cases, people don't get angry over minute nettles. the small problems people stress over are the last jenga block being pulled! my tipping point is greater than what someone else's may be. i innately mitigate my stressors, i don't react to things that upset others. i used to occasionally be called out for it, but i don't mind being so nonchalant. layout to yourself if you are the dry twig, breaking in the breeze. or if you're the nutrient-rich twig, swaying on the tree. take care of yourself, you're the main benefactor in regards to helping you:)
if you find yourself being the dry twig, which reacts to everything that the environment throws your way; do your best to stay grounded, and provide yourself with what's necessary to retain the nutrients that your environment also has to offer. Pour into yourself, and I'm sure you'll find you're more able to withstand the elements:)

And Things of That Nature

nature is unapologetic,
she feels every emotion.
we feel them too.
in tune with our mother's.
the sunny days,
a summertime love - a warm and tight hug.
the calm overcast,
stillness. tranquil. at rest.
we've all napped at one point!
rainy reminders,
it's okay to cry,
eventually those tears must evaporate.
lightning lashes out,
that storm too, must pass.
we hate when mother nature is angry,
why would we ourselves remain angry?

Unapologetic Nature

nature flows
free of worry
free of complaint
nature grows
there's no hurry
or restraints

Harmony

i am one with the wind
only the leaf on the river
dandelions snatched by the swirling gust
snowflakes skiing on the heavily suggestive winds
im admiring life through a tourists' gleam perched upon an open-top bus
my binoculars help me with every detailed observation
i held a shell to my ear and heard nature's conversation
i'm only an ant in the colony
making my way through the hive
im just your average fish
who saw the ocean and dived
behind the wheel i'm still
along for the ride
like my passenger princess who stays by my side
i am evaporation clouded up in the sky;
i said i'm one with the wind
no matter how low or up high
i am the precipitation which tickles your cheeks
pitter-patter percussion, drumming a unique beat
don't mind me
easy to say as the flowing water beneath your feet

Sol

her name is sol which is very fitting
she touches the souls of the beings she's in the presence of
good luck ignoring her, she's a star
the center of attention
the center of a system
the star the earth orbits
sol's consistent which i'd consider thoughtful
not to mention, rather bright, intelligent, ahead of her time
no.
right on time!
in fact, just in time for me to appreciate her beauty.
she showers me with warmth.
in turn, i shower her with love
she sends regards below
while i reflect them back above
im really cool, she's hot as hell
we complement each other well

The Life of Butterflies

a butterfly can't see its own wings
yet it can trust itself to fly
don't doubt your capabilities
simply for eluding your eyes
what you can't see,
or appreciate in yourself
may be the same thing we love
and wish we had for ourselves
we're our biggest critics
self-praise just isn't promised
when we receive compliments we must listen
understand they being honest
just cause we can't see it doesn't mean they're lying
sometimes it's out of view
or we're not trying
to hear what's needed,
blinded by our myopic truths
the butterfly's biggest curse
is not having the vision
to see its worth or even beauty
it doesn't know why it captures attention
having done nothing to gain your bounty
you simply existed and the world loved you
your beauty is your wanted poster
la vida de las mariposas

Love:

I consider myself a hopeful romantic, I find myself often romanticizing life and the different facets of it, whether it's the people around me or merely the conversations I have with myself. I truly believe love makes the world go round. I often write about a romantic love but I put the same passion into my platonic relationships as well. If we poured our love into the community the same way we do when we're in love - with our partners, with the ones we so eagerly long for, with our crushes - how could our communities look? These are some poems which can only begin to describe my love. No amount of words can truly capture what I have to give.

L.O.V.E.

i feel like the word love is overused
i hardly know what love means to me
but i'd love to know what love means to you
i want to hold you tighter than your eyes when you sneeze.
physical touch is the language i speak
quality time is the language i seek
that looks like a kiss on the cheek
like my eyes resting on my eyelids
you're the most beautiful place my sight has laid
L.O.VE. is
Laws Of Vibrational Energy
ur wavelength matches mine
L.O.V.E. is
Lots Of Violent Emotions
and lovely explosions in the heat of the moment
like when our lust lashes out livening commotion
or the waves crashing from the motion in the ocean
L.O.V.E. is when you
Listen, Observe, Visualize, Express
emphasis on the last one because you have the rest
see, you could feel the world but leave it all on ya chest
that's contribution to late nights when you struggle to rest
you and i together is me at my best
you as fly as birds no matter how you be dressed
cool as the other side of the pillow no matter how you be stressed
its a different type of peace when your lips and mine are pressed
L.O.V.E is
Loyalty Out Values Everything
when you feel the world is against you,
you can count on me for anything, i promise

i'm loyal til the end;
death before dishonor

I Care For You The Best Way I Know How

i make playlists for you cus i know you like listening to curated music
i skip certain songs in the car cus i know you don't like an artist or a song
i remove songs in my queue for you
i turn your seat warmer on before i pick you up so your seat isn't cold
i hold the door for you cus you shouldnt be bothered with touching it
i make you soup when you're sick, cus soup was given to me when i was sick
i write down what you tell me so i can remember it later on
sometimes i'm hard on you cus i want the best for you
i eat the foods you enjoy so i can get a taste for your palate
i smell the candles you use so i can get you some new ones
i'll learn anything you're passionate about so i can share not only my world but yours too
whenever you speak i'll close my mouth as i want to hear everything you have to say
i'll give you your distance cus sometimes i need it too
and i don't mind when you're clingy cus sometimes all i want is you
i'd learn you're love languages so i knew how to love you

When I Love, I Love Hard

i give you my all to make up for how long i've given only to myself
i may trip, but i won't fall; i'm perpetually stumbling
who cares if i make a fool of myself if i get you to laugh out loud
i could disappoint the world to make you proud
i'd be lying if i told you i haven't been hurt before
but after all the healing i've had much more to gain
i recognize you must be worth the pain i've sought never to put myself through again
because through my sorrows of yesterdays
i've learned new ways to approach tomorrows and todays
you have a way of speaking my language like no one else
or maybe there's no one else i'd want to understand more
so your language is my second tongue,
we're confluent
i'd practice with every breath in my lungs
to prove i'm fluent
i want the type of love that makes me write a poem about you
cus i can't help but to express how much i love you
i want the type of love when i know her patterns
and the she knows mine
when i don't need to ask what's the matter
because we're aligned
you don't have to say the words, they're tugging at the back of my mind
because i know you, and you know me
we are not halves;
but two wholes meeting at once
we're capable on our own
but together we're a force to be reckoned with

Pedals & Thorns

rose, how i love your pedals
your scent calls me by name
but your thorns tell me you're dangerous
maybe it's best i stay away
look, but don't touch;
i've tried to hold you,
my hands don't fit between your thorns
who am i to harm you
and force you to conform
i'll tend to your needs
until someone else is here
whose fingers fit your thorns
who may love you without concern
i'll water you as the rain
and keep the insects off your pedals
your beauty shines through clouds of gray;
in any conditions and/or weather
thank you for allowing me to care for you,
i have loved you as my own.
i hope i did enough for you
i'll still love you when you're gone.
when your person comes to take you home
i'll love you enough to let you go

Acquainted Lips

when our lips meet it's always like the first time
every pullback is an opportunity to reacquaint once again
inviting the feeling of the last time
my favorite form of communication is the exchange of DNA

Being/Social Media

her presence
her atmosphere
her essence
how just appearing makes an entrance
is posting you're s/o really the epitome
the socials got the youth confused
your appreciation stems from action
superior to the act of reposting posts
i feel no pull to post her picture to my story truly
a photo couldnt capture her entire beauty

Life of Chivalry

too many times i've heard chivalry died
i've been keeping it alive, so somebody's lying
i don't claim to be perfect, but i claim to be trying
let me interject; reviving a sport that's dying
i'm washingtonian, born and raised
so i don't get affected; only bored by rain
i keep an umbrella for her and walk her pace
i'd be jealous if the rain ever kissed her face
holding the door is a common routine
i tend to her needs cus i'm part of her team
i don't need to be in love to do all of these things
it comes naturally for servants to cater to queens
chivalry's personified vicariously through me
not only a queen;
alas my passenger princess
behold a beautiful being
i found her name off santa's nice list
i give her my time instead of gifts;
appreciation is priceless
i wear my jacket until it's her turn
i'm my own priority, but she comes first
that's a double entendre, i can confirm
when i see her goosebumps that's my concern
at the end of the day... it's night
i'm a hopeful romantic
i love leaving her notes i write
it's a part of my antics
some consider me dated
that's opinionated so i don't mind it
chivalry's underrated

what i do is timeless
if it truly were dead
i surely revived it

My Perfect Woman

my perfect woman doesn't have a physical body
yet she outweighs every thought in mind
she's a simple void,
i find myself always looking to complete the picture
it's strange, i have to sense her
without my eyes i can see her
i'll know who she is,
i'd recognize her in any lifetime
she speaks as though her words were handcrafted for me
she walks with a tenderness causing the roses around her to rise out of
a wilting gloom
mother nature herself approves
her kindness takes flight among the birds in true tranquillity
and showers everyone around her with it
i'd be a fool to be jealous;
everybody loves her, not just me

What Is Love

love can sound mean;
but love wouldn't tear you down
love may correct you
but love wouldn't overwrite you

Meant 2 Be

you're where i run to when i'm homesick
all the company i need when i get lonely
the place i lay my head when i'm fatigued
you're my favorite book to read
your body's my favorite language
my job's to stay fluent
every word you have is sacred
you're steering the wheel
i'm the vehicle
you're driving me crazy
you're my glasses; necessary to aid my vision
the first thing i reach for each morning
i'll be your journal, a safe space
as your secret would be
you're safe with me
as pb is to j
as o is to k
we belong together
like pineapple on pizza

Hold Me

i need someone to hold
someone to keep close
and one day we'll grow old
i wanna hold your hand
so i can walk with my eyes closed
i trust your guidance
so why would i need mine
we know trust falls
i've already fallen for you
this is a trust walk
where i hold your hand in mine
close my eyes
taking it step by step
knowing i'm in good hands

Appreciate Me

i want you to love me like you'll never get another chance
hold me like my body is another hand
feel me like a rhythm when you wanna dance
adore me like you'll never have another man
don't ever treat me like a backup plan
i want you too
but recognize i'm not here to beg
when i put you first then i expect the same
if you can't reciprocate me that's a shame
i don't know if you'd say the same but i want you in my life
what i'll do once i'll do again
so you can count on me like a number line
i want to adventure with you like i'm lost at sea

My Mind Has A Room For You

my mind has a room for you
cus you're there all the time
even if you're not at the forefront
you're at the back of my mind
you're always welcome
without hesitation
you can book a room
without reservation

Following My Heart

i will not deny or denounce my love for you
whether you choose to reciprocate,
accept,
or simply acknowledge
it's not in my control
i'm under its' command
and i will devote my life to its leadership

A Pure Mug

i wouldn't dare to say true love has died
rare it may be,
but i know it's real cus i'm alive
i know when you love yourself fully and unselfishly
there's a constant pull to love others
consider yourself a mug
and the kettle is full of love
you may choose to pour into others,
but eventually you'll be left empty,
in your goal to pour into others
you're neglected
when you pour into yourself,
you don't have to worry about never filling up the way you wish to
instead of the sediment of worry you once had
you'll realize it's buoyant, and as your mug fills
worry rises to the top
soon it spills over and out
now that you're overfilled,
you will continue to overflow
but as your overflow ensues,
you'll notice your cup is pure
from here on out,
anytime you pour love into yourself
your love flows not only through you
but back into the world
flowing through others,
flowing through nature
flowing authentically
you will never again be drained of love
it will never be a chore

as long as you continue to love yourself
you'll struggle not to love more

Dear Rose

there's no sacrifice being gracious
having a strength so intense
you make vulnerable look courageous
an act stronger than your defense
not described as dainty,
beauty she has,
defenseless she isn't
she holds attention captive
attractive bold crimson
fragrance full of pleasure;
not for me, but for herself
she's attained the world's treasure
if her knowledge were her wealth

I'll Love You When You Won't

love yourself is plastered around the world
it's a good message
i know sometimes it's hard to do just that
to think we could love our biggest critic
even if you couldn't stand to love yourself
i would overcompensate

Love Starts With Me

searching the world for whom i love would take
too long
so i became the person whom i love
every moment with myself
is another moment at home

What's My Type?

i like a woman who likes to read, likes to write, likes to learn, and likes to love.
i like a woman who knows more than the people around her.
i like a woman who is caring, she's there for herself, for her friends, & for me.
i like a woman like this because this is the character of someone you would move mountains for.
i like a woman who's clear with her boundaries and decisive in her desires.
i like a woman who knows what she wants but is chill enough to go with the flow.
can be stern, can be playful, but most importantly faithful.
i want a woman i like, cus when i like you i naturally cater to you.
it might seem crazy; i apologize cus i can't help that i care for you the best way i know how.
and if you got a better way i want to know it.
i want a love that flows like waterfalls not dams

You're Vital For Me

you're my flesh, you're my blood
you are the heart that makes me pump ￼
you are the air in my lungs
if you left me i'd be breathless
not quite the same way as when we first met
i don't want to squander the wonderful opportunity to wander where wonder roams
i yearn for long-term;
im not content bringing you home for fun
i wanna stargaze, play card games, & bathe in the sun
i wanna venture wherever, stuck together as gum

My Love

my love isn't perfect but it is boundless
it needs correction, colors out of the lines,
but makes homes of houses
my love is forever changing; always adjusting to the shape of you
for you i'd roll the rock of sisyphus to the very top
to keep your world from crashing down, i'd take atlas' job
my love is loyal
i'm in your corner more than darkness
death could only make my love for you eternal
if you're a climber, i'm your harness
i'll be your pen for you to journal
i'll leave you with kisses and i'll greet you with hugs
because that's what comes to mind; thinking of love

Our Garden of Love

roses are red
violets are blue
i feel much better
when i'm next to you
lavender smells good and tulips are yellow
your energy's pure and you make me feel mellow
you appear in my sweet dreams
all pleasure like sweet peas
an innocent smile white as the pedals of daisies
a world without you in it spins my head too crazy
your elegance sprouts orchids
making the walls i've built forfeit
i sure hope there's no danger
my heart feels your hydrangeas
i cherish our friendship, we have lots of fun
your optimism blooms of chrysanthemums
i vow to stand by you to never lose your trust
that could turn a strong foundation to a pit of dust
i'd rather not go down the hill
keep on dancing you dandy daffodil
our dishonesty's rare that's a lack of lies
if i ever lied once i'd correct it twice that
with a brand new flower for our garden; lilacs
today's culture may instill fear in ya
but my loyalty's as real as the alstroemeria
i admire you not faking
i live with the fascination of a carnation

Silence Is My Love Language

at times, i'd rather observe
sit back and watch as the world goes on
i don't always need to have the last word
in fact sometimes i don't want to give you a word at all
i want to sit quietly taking in everything you have to share
i wanna see how you fill these spaces of silence
do you adapt and keep it cool
or are you lost
in need of my words
how's your reliance?
are you independent?
able to hold your own?
so well off you wonder what you need me for?
i look for how you handle your own
if you couldn't handle yourself
you couldn't handle me
i'm not looking to burden you with my presence
so i won't do too much
but sit in silence,
overthink,
and observe.

Confined Butterfly

i understand being the pillar;
the constant need to be tough
but i don't mind being the butterfly
who's sensitive to the touch
while a solid foundation sets the tone for security
i'd rather walk through a park holding hands in vulnerability

One of The Same Tongue

one of the same tongue
a beat from the same drum
we're in unison, if in you's a son
then i can't wait to be a father
i can't wait to have a daughter
i wanna build a household
and i want to hold a partner
im over will and jada, no martin and gina, bonnie and clyde
for all it's worth to me they could've all been alike
cus i don't want it if there's a love truer than yours and mine
if i say the first part, then you'll likely say the second
i know you like my bible if ever i was the reverend

Everything Good

these are the things that remind me of you
autocorrect working after misspelling a word
finding the last puzzle piece after thinking it was missing
sigh of relief
the gasp of air after swimming underwater
checking your bank account after getting your paycheck
having your meal paid for by the person in front of you
the end of the rainbow
getting a good score on a test you didnt study for
the campfire on a cold night

The Raindrop To My Prescription

the raindrop to my precipitation
i've fallen for the rain
the prescription for my glasses
crystal clear like window panes
she's something like the sun to me
and i guess i'd be her earth
i find myself in orbit
but that path is much preferred

Too Similar

its dangerous letting myself get so close to someone who reminds me of me
reason being
if i hold myself to the highest standard i expect it from you too
the love i have for myself transfers so fluidly into the way i love you
seeing the similarities i have with you changes the way i view you
it might be selfish but
i want to take care of you cus how could i neglect myself
you're 1.5 people to me cus although i'm a whole person you're still my other half
that's where you got me at
its a curse to think you're perfect

Your Love Is A Concert

taking place on the stage.
arranging an entrance.
we exchange our presents,
we engage in our presence.
its just us in attendance
you tug the strings of my heart,
the way musicians pluck the strings of guitars.
i imagine a cord by the hearth,
or bored together under the stars.
my mind wonders,
waiting for you to pick it apart
i'm curious if you've mastered the piano.
the keys don't just strike cords,
they do what they want to,
keys unlock many doors,
your keys unlock my love too,
time lost, thinking of nothing but you.
time spent, thinking of something so true.
but overall overthinking us two
the heart is the percussion.
beating in sync with your direction.
my answers to your questions,
the concert of connection,
sold out tickets,
in the arena of affection.
the curtains closed
the lights turn cold
i hope that you enjoyed the show
the first show ends,
tour begins.

i hope together we grow old.

Evol:

It's not quite love, but it's worth talking about. A backwards love if you will. The antithesis of true love; it's evil; evol.

Thorns & Pedals

rose, how i love your pedals
your scent calls me by name
but your thorns tell me you're dangerous
maybe it's best i stay away
every time i hold you
i lose a little more blood
yet i don't let go;
is a bandage enough?
again i reach out to you,
again i pay the price
i don't want to choose
between loving and life
whether i love you for your rose
or hate the thorns which impale
im left choosing dying for you
or living to tell the tale

We Don't Speak The Same Language

i was happy to meet someone like you
sad to find we fit like two left shoes
you're the puzzle i put together
excited about completion
only to get closer
finding out you're the missing pieces
i'm the king, you're not the queen i thought you were
you're the joker in the deck of 52 cards
the card which makes you scream til your lungs are hurt
the one you should've discarded
the one that plays you when put in play
you're the line that splits the heart
to complete the puzzle,
maybe i'll use one of those pieces
you disguised yourself as the queen bee
i'm the bee that tracks the nectar to your sweetness
you're the bear who destroys colonies for honey
extra reckless when you're hungry
you're the oil to my h20
no matter how close we are we just don't mix - even on a molecular level
you're the pain to my pleasure
do opposites attract?
or were we all too similar?

Don't Love Me When It's Convenient

don't love me when it's convenient;
love me when it's not.
love me in all phases, times of the day, and places
love me through your anger;
love me through the hard times;
love me despite it
unconditionally; not only when you feel like it
don't love me casually, but as if love came to you naturally
this won't work if loving me is a chore
there's no one way love looks or acts;
there's no guide for what is good, nor what's bad
love feels like choosing your courses and getting into all of them
love feels like getting something from a vending machine and two items falling
love feels like when someone misses the shot and the ball rebounds to you
love feels like a reward that you didn't have to work for
love feels like your teammate spiking the ball after a long rally
the triumph, sense of joy; the longer it lasts the more exciting it gets
every secret, shared experience, and connection strengthening the bond
love feels like laying in bed after moving around all day - tension leaves and muscles relax
a breath of fresh air
love feels like the calm in the eye of the storm
even in the midst of chaos my arms are your place of peace
because if anything got to you it must've already gone through me
i can be protective but i will always have a soft spot for you
and that's why trusting you is key
i can only be destroyed from the inside

the only thing that could tear me down is you
love may look like passion - a variety of flavor
energies intense - with admiration, joy, or anger
love is through the ups and downs.
love may differ the next morning like the stock exchanges
but it's a gamble and the risks are worth the danger

This Can't Be Love

i tell myself it's better
if i just let her be
she'll be fine by herself
i gotta focus on me
got her own goals and dreams
i'm just not what she needs
i'd be slowing her down
i bring myself up to speed
but when i close my eyes she's all that i see
that's when i start envisioning her future with me
just sitting in her presence i'm feeling at peace
like if i were a boat she'd be the calmest of seas
if she were with me i'd fulfill every need
to start the pretty tree, i try to plant a little seed
but the soil has to want it, i'm just not what she needs
i wonder if it's love but that just couldn't be
this can't be love
one sec i can't get enough
the next i wanna give up
this can't be love
i know times can be rough
but this a little too tough
this can't be love
i'm reaching new kinds of lows
more goodbyes than hellos
this can't be love
i've lost all my hope
i keep my eyes stuck above
this can't be love
i got my own things to do

i tell me brotha move on
write another poem
sing another song
expand on your ideas,
just leave her alone
but without her not a house that ever feel like a home
i feel like a dog who went to fetch for a bone
i've retrieved it now i'm realizing there's no one to throw
solitude is cool but now i'm always alone
changing my habits; we'd fit together as one
C-Mo she don't give a damn about what you doin
not every single human has an obsession with union
you don't gotta give your all, what's the point that you provin'
leave it all on the line but it's yourself that you're losing
this can't be love
i wonder what we could be
i think it's best if i leave
this can't be love
i say she's all that i need
but that's tuff to believe
so i don't get my relief
this can't be love
it's like we competing
but on different teams
i tend to think in extremes
we start to feel like a dream
this can't be love
the reason i write; there's a lot on my mind
how's the world going to change if i don't put in the time
i got people to help
some living, some dying
but if change starts with me

i needa stay on my grind
damn it's hard to focus there's a lot on my mind
i spend too many hours wanting her to be mine
she must be bad for my health
but i feel so alive
its like i found the deep end, got careless,
and dived
wrong versus right
my heart vs my mind
i think it's time i set my feelings aside
this can't be love
i got my own things to do
though i'm so focused on you
what's a brotha to do
this can't be love
she makes gray skies of blue
she makes lies of the truth
she makes a blend of the hues
this can't be love
she makes my sureness confused
and my acceptance refused
i'm not entertained
while she looks so amused
this can't be love

The Little Things

many speak of the importance of the little things
anybody can do grand gestures
but who does what others haven't done already
helping me get in touch with my emotions was your doing
even though being open to it was solely my choosing
i wondered how and why i let myself do that before you said "bye"
it was refreshing meeting you because when it's genuine it's hard to come by
even when i fell silent without a clue what to say
i listened because i could listen to you talking all day
you taught me how to feel
and then you broke my heart

Until Next Time

goodbye, she says
see you later, i reply
hoping this isn't bye for good
but a minor delay in the next time i'll see her
maybe if i hold my blink
she won't be gone as long
i appreciate our connection,
we seem to have a knack for feeling each other
until we reunite,
i'll feel her absence

Stuck in My Thoughts

you're trapped in my mind
both of us are helpless
while in your reality you're free
in my mind you're stuck with me
no matter how many times i try to let you go
you cannot escape my thoughts
i guess i'm stuck with you too

Gone With The Wind

momentarily she had my heart
then she was gone with the wind
she made me feel whole again,
even if only for a second

To Love & Be Loved

i'm content on my own
but sometimes it hurts to be alone
not for a lack of love
its quite polar
i have so much love to give that'd i spoil her
but there's no 'her' to give this world to
when you have this much love to give
it becomes overwhelming
i need someone to love
i'm motivated by my acts of service
romantically i have no one to serve
but i can't give my heart to anyone
i need someone who deserves it
how could such a positive love
feel so negatively overwhelming
so much joy it's sadness
so much love it's heartbreak
reciprocation is the only bandage
that could heal this heartache
i want someone who reciprocates me
shows me they're worth my time
i want to feel appreciated too
it's not for a lack of trying
in search, i'd give my last dollar
but many i've found weren't worth a dime
i'm a hopeful romantic
well,
fully romantic, but i'm losing hope
i know love exists
because i know my heart

but finding someone else like me?
i wouldn't know where to start
a love this genuine
ignores the circumstances
unconditional until the very end
my love will outlast my existence
otherwise it'd meet conditions

Foresight

i hope i have the foresight
to recognize the people i'll miss
before i miss them

Found & Lost

i haven't been searching
but now that i've found you
you'll be missing

Fatal Attraction

it seems no matter how bad for me you are
i make exceptions

I’m Sorry, I’m Growing

i’m sorry i want to show you my roses and not my buds
i’m sorry that my thorns keep you farther from my love
i’m not keeping you at arms out of fear or disgust
i’m only human, my thorns outpace my trust
if we were meant to be
i wouldn't have to harm myself to hold you
you’re worth the break of a thorn
i’ll force myself to conform
i may bend but i don't break
there’s a sunny day in the eye of the storm
even amidst the chaos
i appreciate that you want to be with me for the process,
the thorns on my stem explain the harm in my progress
i’m rising as a rose, but my thorns still grow in excess
come see me when i’ve grown but know my growing will be endless.
i can pain myself for love
or understand i’ve outgrown you
i’d love to love you without restraint
to know we don’t clash
because we grow as one
i’m going through things i can’t explain
if you’re growing too you could understand
but if that’s the case
we may be able to grow together yet

She Wants Her Heart Mended Too

she gave him her time
and he counted the minutes
she spoke her mind
and he wouldn't listen
she said she loved him
but she loved his potential
does he not think twice about the hate he breeds?
like a woman didn't give him life and is why he breathe?
she put her trust in him
he showed her why that was a bad idea
she showed no one love but him
while he ignored her existence
cus who could possibly be more important than you?
it's mighty audacious to want her now
after she felt like an option
she didn't care to pursue him
that's what caught his attention isn't it?
he tried the same tactics
told her this time it's gonna be different
but she's read this story before
and know how it ends
no thank you she says,
careful not to break the eggshells she walks on
he can't take rejection
everything she does for herself feels like a shot at him
how dare she live to fulfill herself
but i must ask you;
how is her concern for her well-being a shot at your pride?
he feels entitled
she told him how she felt

he struggles with reception
she said she doesn't want sex
he thought he should be the exception
he's angry at a woman 'cus she not submissive
he start to get upset and then he get aggressive
she don't belong to him but still he got possessive
she invites him to leave, and he refuses
as if the decision is up to him
"what about my broken heart!?" he proclaimed
"where would i start?" she would say
"how about the things i've been through!?" he yelled
like he wasn't dragging her through hell
"i feel pain too!" he hollered
as he grabs her by the collar
he always made sure she felt his pain
"i have a broken heart!" he vented
her feelings unattended to
she had no words she cared to mention
she wants her heart mended too

Untitled:

Not every poem needs a name, these also tend to be the shorter poems, but I'm not going to delve into the obvious. Some of these were a string of thoughts i wrote down before i had the chance to forget.

where words fail me
my poems will honor my every thought

...

i'll be your snowman;
then it won't only be my heart which melts when i see you

...

what impresses me is who you are,
not what you have

...

your absence is an entity i feel so thoroughly

...

mosquito stay away
when it's you and i
know i choose me
utshamelessly
you chose me too

...

every time i feel content alone
you make your presence felt
again i'm reminded why i can't live without you

...

someone else may be able to narrate your story,
but only you can write it

...

normal isn't a standard

everything's weird to somebody

...

there's no greater motivator than yourself.
it's your decision each day to get up and do the hard part

...

i realized time was a social construct
when i started working weekends

...

every time we allow an exception
we create a new standard
a lower standard

...

i'd rather be heartbroken by truth
than believe love lies

...

don't feel guilty for setting your boundaries,
you deserve to have peace

...

i may not be what you came for
but i'll be the reason you stay

...

systems of authority
only work as well
as the integrity of its leadership allows for

...

i love the way a camera can capture a moment
i want my words to do the same thing

...

can we take a moment
to endorse healthy expression

...

her looks were intoxicating

i stared as though i hated sobriety

...

circling the corrupt government in red
not only symbolic for the blood they've spilled
but to bring attention to their need for correction

...

in a world so negative
she maintained such an infectious positivity
wilting flowers stood tall in her presence
as if they never lost their glow

...

ai won't love you like i will
as intelligent as it may be
it wouldn't love you in any way
aside from artificially

...

i'm sorry if my eyes are closed to you
i hope i don't look back wishing they were open then

...

your intention doesn't excuse your action

...

i have limitless words to tell you
and limited context to get them out

...

ironically,
the comfort zone makes me uncomfortable

...

your words are worth listening to

...

sometimes i fall out of love from distance
am i in love with you or our proximity
am i really in love with you

or have i simply romanticized your presence

...

i always said not with that attitude
to offer you a moment to change your mind
a simple fact is
if you continue to believe that
you'll continue to achieve that

...

contentment isn't conditional
it's being okay regardless of your circumstances
even when you don't want to be in them

...

forgive the long explanation;
i'm still figuring it out

...

moon,
if only you knew how excited people are when they see you

...

even if i don't define the conditions
i refuse to let the conditions define me

...

if the strongest voice is opposition
they'll never hear you out

...

i'll love you through every season
all different phases

...

i never miss you until i see you again

...

we're all broken looking for something to heal us
so don't use your brokenness to break more people
their broken pieces won't fix yours

...

how do we plan to fight war with violence
do we drown the noise with silence?
instead of destruction for mitigation
what if we sought peace for mediation
we formed strong relations
instead of fighting with arms
we settle down through conversation

...

when food drops
the floor is well-fed

...

dear mama
thanks for your patience
i promise to return on your investment
thank you for waiting

...

i say i'm an open book
but forget to mention
you can flip through all my pages
some weren't written
i have nothing to hide
something's missing
you can't lay vision
on what i forget to write

...

i hate your resistance
but i'm loving the friction

...

they say money can't buy you happiness
but if freedom to you equates to happiness
that can be bought

if you have the money to stay home
and spend time with family
then happiness can be bought

...

i'm top 3
not 3
not 2
but don't get confused
i'm not the 1 to play with

...

your beauty is unconditional

...

you wouldn't survive a day in my mind
its not meant for you
you couldn't be me if you wanted to
lost in this maze, the only guide is me
but if i had your mind
i couldn't help you either

...

hard to see your red flags,
with those rose-colored lenses
you either love me or you don't
quit balancing on fences

...

it almost hurts how much i think about you
my passenger seat is empty
so my brain fills in the gaps
my phantom passenger princess
and you don't even know it

...

i don't play an instrument but that's okay i don't need one

i'm freestyling life to the beat of my own drum

...

i treat my inner child like a son of mine
how could i not want the best for him
i'm all for my own growth
but i put him first as any father sh~~w~~ould

...

its that time of year again,
when moon becomes the early bird
sun begins sleeping in
moon wakes up much earlier

...

when i spend time with my thoughts i wonder what we could be
am i blinded for my love for you or are you all i see?
my mind is racing,
going places,
i want you here with me

...

in the heat of the moment
cold doesn't stand a chance

...

my mind and heart are in a relationship
as any healthy relationship goes
decisions are decided by both partners
the mind doesn't move without a pulse
my heart doesn't make a choice
my feelings are strong but i need to justify myself
the logical decision may not be the one that feels right

...

you have to push others to be their best
what do we gain by being at our worst
except the motivation to be better

...

looks can only take you so far
what's really attractive is who you are

...

you don't know what you'd do if you were me
you know what you'd do given my position
you don't know the first thing about being me
would you really tie my shoes and walk the same conditions?
name anything about me;
any three things
my life may look easy;
it's the difficult you won't see

...

when i fell for you, gravity slammed me down
i fell so hard i broke the ground
after standing up, i looked around
attraction no longer leaves me bound to you
the force of the fall must've shaken something inside me

...

i'm always excited for the future
due to how i live in the present

...

even in low times i keep my head up
keeping my eyes focused on where i'm headed

...

as the world were to be engulfed by flames,
i would sit by idly roasting marshmallows
and as the smoke bellows i'd fuel its density
to choke the world cus anger hosts no empathy
~ written in anger ~

...

count me out if you like

imma keep on counting

...

with everything i spent this week
i could have had gas & groceries

...

i live for when you impulsively love me
on a whim
it makes me feel seen

...

i lived another day on this earth
that's a reason to celebrate

..

i wanna learn without the statistics
don't tell me how many i got wrong
just let me know i need practice
im not worried about my percentile
my competition is myself yesterday

...

content with less
if we yearn for everything
we'll always end up wanting more

...

i've seen dogs bite the hand that feeds him
bears who have asked for fish but never a fishing rod
parrots who've asked for a solution but never how to solve problems
horses led to water and dehydrated by pride
i've watched birds fly to the flock that got shot just to fit in a crowd
possums play dead until a car comes and it's no longer a game
you better be willing to be about what you joke about

...

i don't take advice
if i wouldn't trade places in life

advice is what you give when you've been there
if you haven't been there,
you can't tell me about how to get there
everything sounds good until you're trying it for yourself
and hindsight is 20/20
but when you're going through it, things are becoming blurry
mike tyson said everybody got a plan until you get punched in the mouth
so if you haven't been in a fight never having been punched is implied

...

a goal of mine is to only have first-world problems; it wouldn't be a problem

...

i wish you could take a field trip into my mind
i'd change your perspective;
its tough for me seeing you so hard on yourself
if you saw through my eyes what i see in you.
you'd respect it

...

im thankful for the days i had nothing to eat
the days when i'd be starving every couple of weeks
i often irritate when i recognize;
it seems life costs more when you're poor
when i spend less, the more i afford

...

i have a homie who say he can't be himself around women
ironically i don't quite feel like myself when i'm with him

...

nobody wants you to grow more than you
its a bigger problem if they do
who'll put more time into your life than you?

...

life has been treating me with deference

...

i don't just write to pass the time i also write to free my mind
though i don't carry pen and paper most my thoughts deserve a line
a place for them to harbor where in darkness they may shine

...

if you really want something in life, fight for it
but give yours, you don't need to take life for it
sacrifices without vices produce pretty surprises

...

i think the way to a better life derives from ways of better thinking

...

the way you use words makes any sentence worth reading

...

you were squeaking from the bleachers
i was preaching to the leaders
questioned why the food belongs to the king
when it's the people who need feeding
i guess he's power-hungry
it's a facade to think you're god
saying "no one's above me"

...

some people treat you based on the things you can do for them

...

mistakes are how we learn, so why do we fear them?

...

people are so busy saying what doesn't need to be said
they don't hear what needs to be heard

...

my regrets are just unanswered questions.
questions i never asked.

...

i trust no man who neglects himself

...

you'll never know what you're capable of until you try

...

there's no room for growth in the comfort zone

...

thinking better about yourself leads to better results
excess stress causes your body to attack itself

...

your want for a result has to be greater
than your lack of want to do the work
required for said result

...

i wake up so excited to begin the day
the night before i'm stuck between
being excited to sleep
and being too excited to sleep

...

hitting snooze is such a funny concept to me
if you won't wake up once,
you likely won't wake up twice

...

i believe the reason we don't get past our feelings
is because we don't allow ourselves to feel them fully

...

i don't claim to have all the answers,
but we won't have answers if we don't ask questions

...

it's funny how a sinner uses god as a last resort
believers use god when they alas retort
it's almost olympic how they pass the torch

...

i hate being lonely;
taking longer showers just to once again feel warmth

...

she has an unforgettable beauty

...

i don't know that i 'believe in fate'
but i feel that there may be a reason for everything
even though we can change an outcome

...

if you're able, go above and beyond

...

maybe he's not gone,
merely living with the dead

...

this feels like the wrong era to be a hope~~less~~ful romantic

...

i don't gamble,
but betting on myself
is winning odds

...

if you're willing to send it around
don't be afraid when it comes back around

...

stop taking on unnecessary obligations
prioritize yourself

...

the true beauty of the moon
is only captured by the organic eye

...

we grow inure to what we encounter most
unless we otherwise force ourselves to recognize it
this is the only hope against comfort and complacency

...

be willing to keep trying.
don't be discouraged when you don't "get it perfect",
when you get better than you did before,
you're getting closer to complete;
perfection.

...

Perfect /ˈpərfək(t)/

1. having all the required or desirable elements, qualities, or characteristics; as good as it is possible to be.
2. make (something) completely free from faults or defects, or as close to such a condition as possible.

- Oxford Dictionary

i'm afraid we've skewed our idea of perfect to be something we couldn't/haven't already achieved

...

you'll never have the right words
for someone who doesn't care to listen to you

...

you can't save anybody if you can't save yourself

...

if people put time into what they said they couldn't do,
the same way they put time towards their desires,
they wouldn't say they couldn't do it

...

live life to the fullest
tomorrow is always a day away and it's not promised

...

does what we put out into the world
affect how we receive the world and/or vice versa?

...

they say without risks, there's no reward...
then what are we doing?
take risks!

...

when i die
no longer there to comfort your tears
don't fear when the rain pours
it's me crying with you

...

i fell into a silence
when everybody halted their conversation
to hear my voice
they ceased their ideas, visions, and thoughts
to hear mine
said they did it out of respect
but all i felt was neglect,
i had nobody to engage
so i too fell silent

...

they ask me why i never cry
i guess i'm not hydrated
i believe in expression
maybe some things i should hide
now i'm downing bottles - of water
so my feelings can roll down my cheek
the way they're supposed to

...

in the grand scheme of things we are so small
but you wouldn't ask another driver to not pay attention to their own lane
so i understand if you don't pause to look around

to see that even the road isn't the only thing in front of us

...

in sadness, i feel at home
the familiar feeling
openly embracing me
in this weather
my tears race the rain
they fall all the same

...

the multitude to which i will feel your absence
may prove to be a larger entity than
the thought of your presence

...

when we see things as a kid they feel huge
when we revisit them later in life...
they feel much smaller
i think it's a testament;
what we're facing now
won't seem so big to us when it's all said and done
at one point in our lives,
the first step was an obstacle
and now we leap and bound up entire staircases

...

i haven't felt the comfort of your arms in quite some time
am i supposed to believe there's safety beyond your reach?

...

i'm scared of you
not in the horrific sense...
terrified of all the lovely possibilities

...

your pleasure's my passion

...

your eyes take me to distant places
places you couldn't see

...

as a poet
i'll get mad at the thoughts i lost
as someone who's self-aware
i find it silly to be mad when i can't even recall what i'm mad at

...

there's nothing more attractive
than watching someone explain their passions
when they have that gleam in their eye
no longer having to think about what they're saying
because the heart is speaking

...

if you're scared to make a mistake
you'll be too worried to grow

...

is the illusion of peace
enough to keep you comfortable?

...

do we not care to be good people anymore?
kindness without expectations around reward
occasionally i'll smile at the acts of kindness on my instagram feed
then wonder if they'd do this without it being on my screen
are they the same without the cameras rolling?
is focus on their channels growing?
is kindness only worth doing when the masses know it?
i'd be damned if i was starving,
and to eat i'd have to be the latest video
i was just looking to eat, now known to the city
if the kindness is for clout it's worse than pity

...

flirting is my favorite dialect

...

i won't allow your evol
to taint my love

...

don't get mad at me for not sharing your anger,
i maintain my peace

...

i am not a failure for failing or even having failed
until i claim my losses as identity i'll be a winner

...

i thought it was a quiet day
i was misguided
i simply couldn't listen beyond my own noise

...

you have my hugs
i have your kisses
let's exchange
in the spirit of christmas

...

trust is a privilege, not a right

...

when you're so adamant about listening and learning, there's so little you need to say

...

it's only the one you count out that sneaks up on you

...

you only have time for what you make time for

...

3 people have an effect on your future:
who you were yesterday,
who you are today,

who you choose to become tomorrow.
all of them rely on who you are today!

...

get inspired!
be referred to as idol, not idle

...

you'll only be taken as seriously
as you take yourself

...

just because you're old doesn't mean you're mature
everybody ages

...

the difference between those who say they'll do something
and those who do something
one tells you about it
the other shows you

...

having a bad attitude is a conscious decision
unless you have no control over your emotions

...

the greatest test of character is that of no punishment and no reward
think: people who return their shopping cart instead of leaving it by their car

...

i appreciate the nights i had no food
the cost of not paying attention was far too expensive
i'm thankful for my experiences of extreme fear
fearing i too could make my way to skid row
not on my own volition, but stuck in a community alike me
without the experiences of being as poor as i'll ever be
there's a chance i'd end up back there

now when i feel hungry i say i'm hungry
thinking back to a time when i knew what it meant to be starving
researching how long i could survive off water alone
you start to realize that sugar isn't just bad for you it's horrible
the fats i was told i'm too skinny to have kept me afloat
when i floundered for food, maybe my next meal
dare i travel elsewhere besides work and home
i'm thankful i knew the feeling of true hunger
because now i'll make sure i never have to feel it again.

...

if not now, when?
the worst action is the absence of it

...

each yes adds a little more weight
when my obligations are too heavy
i'll wonder how much lighter a no could be

...

i try to learn as much as i can before i go
i fear i'll only be heard after i'm gone
i have so much i wish to share before then

...

i knew this was a wicked world
when i was praised for the bare minimum
the average standard is a low standard

...

even baby steps are moving forward
small progress is still progress

...

i'm not necessarily an optimist
but if you never look for the silver lining
you'll never see it

...

siempre te querré
constantly & without shame

...

i still love you like the first time i saw you

...

my love for you is not conditional
so when you decide to come back around
i'll still have this heart of mine
i guarantee it pumps out enough love for the both of us
many things alter as the future turns to past
but my love for you is constant
unlike the seasons which'll pass
i know you love to go around
when you come back
my love for you will have stacked
collecting interest over time
you may indeed make the most significant withdrawal of your life

...

you wove the fabric of love itself
into a web i can't escape
i know better then to squirm
in this case movement could be dangerous

...

the butterflies in my stomach get more excited
at the sight of you than i do
i'll feel the feelings as if they could be my own
but i won't act this way
it's not defiance
i'm simply not compelled enough to act
the same way they are

...

when he writes
his message projected like many mics
i'll describe what its like; helping visualize
mind thinking bout problems theres many types
if we want, we can solve all the many plights
please open your ears and then close your eyes
let my words take you farther like mini flights
make like a kite pursuing brand new heights and
walk the path of the enlightened - it's marvelous
i don't need the presence of the populace
but why i feel like i'm the only body walking this
like your tv isn't on and you aint watching this

...

i have sought my best self for her
becoming better at every chance
so even if we don't pan out
i will
i'll still have all the hours of knowledge on hand
the skills i thought would be useful
i'll prove to myself that they were

...

the glare in her glasses couldnt take the beauty of her eyes away
it seems she too loved them enough to leave them framed

...

it's okay to be sad for a little
but don't let sadness become routine

...

every writer needs a reader
thank you for your time <3

Don't miss out!

Visit the website below and you can sign up to receive emails whenever Caleb C-Mo Morris publishes a new book. There's no charge and no obligation.

https://books2read.com/r/B-A-VUYV-RMBRC

BOOKS 2 READ

Connecting independent readers to independent writers.

Did you love *The Next Step in Evolution*? Then you should read *A Brief Guide By My Mind*[1] by Caleb C-Mo Morris!

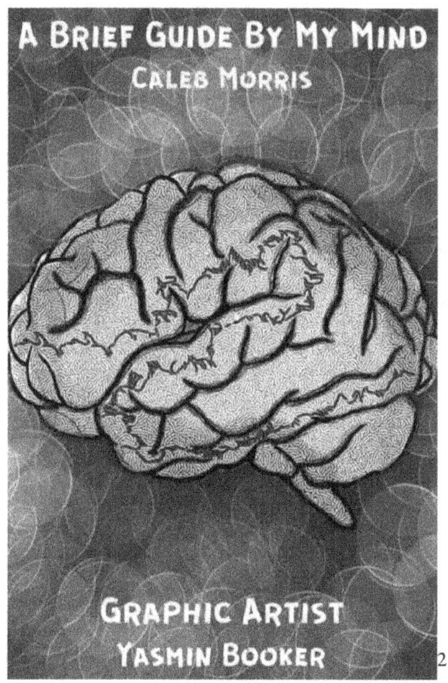

[2]

'A Brief Guide By My Mind' is a collection of poems by Caleb 'C-Mo' Morris. They're all original poems inspired by everyday life, experiences, thoughts, and ideas. Some poems offer relatable perspectives and experiences, others more universal in theme!

Read more at calebamorris.com.

---

1. https://books2read.com/u/m2dajd

2. https://books2read.com/u/m2dajd

About the Author

C-Mo is a poet from Lacey, Washington. He uses his experiences, thoughts, and ideas to engender new poems and leans on his emotions and empathy to create works that can be felt.

Read more at calebamorris.com.

Printed in the USA
CPSIA information can be obtained
at www.ICGtesting.com
JSHW021528311223
54588JS00001B/45